MOMENTS OF AWE

Moments of Awe
©*2024 by Betty Lou Bowles*

Published by **Hobo Jungle Press**
Sharon, Connecticut, USA
St. Vincent & the Grenadines, W.I.

First edition
January 2024

Printed in the United States of America

ISBN #979-8-9897406-0-4
Library of Congress Control Number: 2023952527

Cover Photograph: *Marc Erdrich*

MOMENTS OF AWE

BY BETTY LOU BOWLES

Contents

Preface

I have been writing poetry for more than 20 years, and first came to love writing when my 4th grade teacher said, "Make a story using all of these spelling words."

In June 2017, after many years of writing classes with Lin Northrup, here in Woodbury and others in Key West, I did a show of my poems and the photos that inspired them in the library with two other artist friends: Molly Tate who is an artist working with watercolors and thread and needle on canvas, and Matt Simpson who is a sculptor. All of the offerings were nature themes in celebration of Darwin's 200th Anniversary.

Sometimes there is a moment in a day that captivates me. Writing a poem crystalizes the event. A few words bubble into my brain, I pause turning them over in my mind, and sit in silence with pen poised waiting.

Introduction

When I think of the word Awe, it makes me feel a sense of excitement, a sense of warmth, and yet Awe also means dread, fear, shock and surprise.

Surprise and disbelief — in some of my poems I discover something about myself. Sometimes that excites me. Other times, it shows how much I have fallen short of my self image. There are several poems in this book that I thought did not fit as a "Moment of Awe" and then I reflected on it again and realized that they fit into the type of awe that surprises us.

Sharing my writing with friends, family and strangers over the years has been a gift to help and uplift.
My hope is you will notice your daily moments of awe. We need only look with the eyes of our heart.

The Venerable Oak

I am old
Insects live in my nooks nibbling contentedly
A squirrel family dwells within my hollows
The robins
      Have come back again this spring
      Making a nest in the crook of my arms
I watch now
      Ancient
      Frayed
      And filled with life

Word Painting

Can I word paint
The wispy tips
Supported by fingers
        and arms
Oh so many arms and fingers
        of this beauty
        we call a tree

What do they call to each other

"Winter is coming
Robins
Cardinals and chickadees
Have nested in us
Along with the raccoons again this year
It is good to have a season to rest"

The Leaves

Reaching for the sun,
the leaves
rose together and
cheered
for the warming sun
and chirping birds,

Feeling glad
for the joy of life itself.

Then the rains came
the leaves glistened
their branches dripped
drinking in this liquid sunshine.

Sun and rain sustain life:
leaves, branches, trees, and roots
nourished by nature.

The Grapes

Saved to enjoy traveling
        Given away instead
To a fellow traveler
Whose gratitude
        Flowed from his eyes

A Summer Morning at the Cottage

Waking
	coolness
whispers over my face

Lace curtains
	move to the rhythm
of the waves

Gentle sounds
	of sparrows and robins
	nudge my eyes open
to soft morning light

A smile
	finds my face
	as I look at the sparkling union
of sun and water

The Grace of God

Moving swiftly
I approach the curve
     A leaf skitters across the road
        Veering
        I avoid the leaf
And the runner
Just round the bend

The Glow

"Betty Lou! Come out and look at the sunset!" Peter
shouted excitedly.
Wow! The sky was red.

"Let's go to the airport
Grab a jacket, I've got the keys," Peter urged.

As we approached North Street, three runners were
heading to the open field to see the red sky. We
raced to the top of Upper Grassy Hill Road.

Reds and blues – light and dark; Pinks!
Textures of every sort – dashes of dark blue sky,
vapor trails left behind in the loss of the sun, but
the light remained and reflected on the clouds, hues
never found in a Crayola box.

Light pale blue at the bottom of the horizon; red with
rolling waves of blue-gray washing onto the horizon's
shore along with baby girl pinks turning to the reds
of a teenager dressing boldly. The baby boy blues
turn to the young toddler's OshKosh denim overalls.
A black streak across the blazing red. Where did that
come from? A cloud of blackness among the blazing
lighted sky. Minutes pass, and the sky's brilliance
turns dark. The shade of night is pulled down on
the day.

17

The Dining Room Table

At this moment
I sit at the great oak table
Arms supported on its highly polished surface

Rippling rivers and streams of veins
Arteries and capillaries run through its hefty body
I admire its rough-hewn edges
The smooth and raised grains
Seem to move under my fingertips
The knots like eyes looking back at me
I marvel at its rich
Rusty surface
I marvel at its rough elegance

This table was once a great red oak
Standing tall and majestic
Until
It was hewn
Falling heavily to the ground

Its grandeur
Reborn to be
Appreciated
Inside our sunny home

The Cornfield

It stands bleak and brown
appearing lifeless

Let us look again
as mice and chipmunks store up for winter

Let us watch as the Canada geese
stop to feast on their long flight

Wild turkeys, racoons, deer, caterpillars, and
grasshoppers enjoy what humans have left behind

Tears

Do my tears matter?
        I do not know.
They come unbidden
as our Spirits
share
the grief.

Morning Walk

I walked this morning as the sun
    began its ascent
    into the sky

The moon
    a shadow of its former self
    began setting in the west

A Bobolink flew from its nest in the grasses
    it's white cream buzz cut bobbing along
    as it hopped from one canary reed
    grass stalk to another
    all the time leading my eyes away
    from its hidden nest

A sparrow sang
    a red winged blackbird landed
    on the telephone pole's crossbar
    and listened to its song

Dancing with the grass
    in the newly risen sun
    brisk breezes lifting my skirts
    I opened my arms to welcome this day

Ode to OC

Orange Cat

You are
Often courageous
You offer comfort and consolation
Your calm exterior
Costumes your champion of the weak
Chivalry still lives in the soul
   Of your aged body
You are not submissive
You are not crude
You are not delicate
You stand and defend Althea and Maisel
Against all who do not come in peace

You do not forgive when you have been crossed
And sometimes you bite the hand that feeds you.
You do not let Peter sleep when you deem it's "Time to get up"
Peter is your human in his way and I am your human in others
Peter always feeds you and you accompany him
Down the stony driveway to get
the newspaper in the morning and the mail midday.

My lap is softer
Which you welcome sometimes
With nails extended into my thinly covered flesh.
And for the ear and neck scratching you lean into my hand
Sometimes you lie with your head on my foot as I attempt
To put my socks and shoes on
I reach down to give you the rub that makes you happy
Then you in turn rub my feet with your head to say thank you

You came to us so many years ago.
And waited to be invited in
You were patient waiting for the right time to cross the threshold
We fed you and watched over you
And made sure you had your rabies shot – to keep us all safe
Then the day came and we opened the door
And you stepped cautiously into the house –
Caution had kept you alive
You looked at us and we heard you say
"Nice place, I'd like to stay but it has to be on my terms"

We agreed.
And each day your presence and laughable antics
Have permeated our home
Delight reigned in our caring for each other

Sunset

The western sky fired by the sun
Hangs onto the edge of the world
Blues, reds, pinks, and yellows

Wonder flows
Through silhouetted trees

Seeking

Do not fence me in
or
clip my wings or hobble my feet

My soul
>   will seek to be all that I was created to be
>   exploring the way of light and love
>   of wondering and curiosity and astonishment

I want to see the splendor of you and me
I want to seek the majesty of the trees
>   clouds and stars
I want to marvel at the snakes birds
>   and chipmunks
and
always experience the awe of
>   the night sky
>   the birth of a child
>   the rising sun

Reverberation

Clickety Clack
        Clickety Clack
          Along the tracks

          Boombox Blaring

Captive passengers
            SILENT

'midst the aching cacophony

Clickety Clack
          Clickety Clack

Not Belonging

They were not my friends
Though I knew them
I am okay with not joining
I do not think as they do
We do not share the same values
Being silent
Being in solitude
I begin to know
What really matters

Kindness
Compassion
Gratitude
Smiles
These are my values

Yes, it was okay

Hope

Hope does not ask Reason
What it feels or thinks
Hope is that spark
That ignites life
That does not falter in
The darkness

Hope is what remains
When life wanes
When the breath shortens
When sleep comes
Finally
Hope is
In the everlasting
Eternity of Light

Morning Practice

Feet flat on the rug
enfolded
in the lap
of God
I relax
with the wonder and awe of each breath

Energy and vitality
stream into my lungs
giving life to each cell
replenishing me
for this day

Transition

The air quivers
The hairs on my arms
And neck
Stand tall
I shiver
Alerted inwardly
To the coming
Yet unknown
Life shift

White Oak

Arms raised high in praise
        for the sun and the rain
and the creator of all
        that nurtured my beginning
and guided my moments

Enriched within
        black soil
        I grew
Pushing up through moist dirt
basking in the sun's warm rays
I came to adulthood at thirty
producing my first batch of acorns

Nubs growing
        stretching
        into long arms and
branching Y's
Y's ever spreading from my thickening body
Y   Y   Y
many arms and fingers wiggling in the wind
bowing and praising God
for creating all

Renewal

When fatigue washes over us,
Let us rest quietly warmed in the sunshine.

As our muscles ease, minds slow, and hearts quiet,
our spirits align with the universal order.

Let us return to our center
as the indwelling Sacred whispers
birthing and guiding our days

When We Say Yes to Life

It is good
that our life's path
is hidden from us

For I believe
fear
would strangle us
if we knew God's plan

And yet
with faith and grace
we step onto that invisible path
knowing that each step
is watched over
guided by
our Redeemer
the Man-God
who has shaken
our worldly ways

By His coming
as one of us

I Imagine

Being in your shoes
Wherever we may be
Enjoying the night sky
The beauty of the oak tree
The robins song

I imagine being in your shoes
When the snows cover the ground
Covers the muck of the gap
Between your world and mine

I imagine being in your shoes
As a stranger sees you
His mind caught off guard
"Other" whispers his mind

It is my deepest hope
That the stranger
Will look again
And see himself

For the beauty of this world
Enriches our spirits
Enriches our connection
To one another
Helping us know
All people are equal
members of our
*One Human Family**

*official motto of Key West

Windy October

One hundred,
           no, one thousand
                   no, ten thousand
leaves
waved and cheered

I heard them

Gleefully delighting in
       this crisp, clear, bright fall day

What is Love?

Is it not to cherish
Each person without judgment
Each day for the gifts we receive
Each smile that another bestows upon us
Each difficulty which broadens our soul
Each raindrop that nourishes the earth
Each dog and cat who love all unconditionally?

Is it not to cherish
Each season that graces us with its beauty
The greening of the spring grass
The first swim of summer
The turning of the autumn leaves
The snow of winter
Flowers in their abundant variations?

Is it not to cherish
People colorful, cross, cantankerous
Humans joyful, sad, giving, loving, angry
Those who challenge our way of thinking
Those who welcome us with their open hearts?

What's So Important?

I am too tired
to insist that my idea is
better than yours

Too tired
to discern the best way forward

What does it matter?
What's so important about having it
MY way?

I need to
breathe
and
let go

Touching

Touch me lightly with tenderness.
Touch my arm, my heart, my spirit.

Touch my intellect with words
     that pique my curiosity,
     that invite me to question,
     that open new windows onto our world.

Touch my soul
     by reading poetry, philosophy, and mysticism,
     by singing chants that resonate at our centers,
     by being silent together reading, or resting.

Touch my body with the gentleness of your hand
Touch my face and neck and shoulders

Take me
     into your arms
     and dance slowly with me to the music
     of the crackling fire.

Why Do I Write?

Why do I write?
To capture
The colors of sunset,
The titmouse on the feeder.

Why do I write?
To capture
The moment when
The crocus announces spring
     though a white shawl
      wraps her purple petals.

Why do I write?
To catch the smile
That stopped my heart,
The tears that flowed in sorrow,
     the anguish of death
      and the blessing of Resurrection.

Wholeness

I Stand before you

Whole

In my brokenness

The Trees

The trees whispered to me today while I swam.

"Be still and know," they murmured.
"Be still and know that you are a part of our roots
        even as we are a part of yours."

I stood watching them in the sunlight,
        dancing to the music of the wind.

"Be still and know that you are a part, as we are,
        of the air breathed by a host of humans."

Tranquilly, I float looking upon their majesty.
"Be still and you will know all that is necessary
        for this day is here now".

I nodded my head and thought
"Thank you, again".

The Sea

Today
Foamy surf rolls gently over sand
Jetty and climbing rocks
The briney ocean caresses the beach
Waves repeatedly wash onto shore
Like a human breathing

But
When the storm whips the waves
Thunderously beating the coastline
The air quivers
Anger and fury inhabit the raging squall
Windows rattle and shutters shake
Like a child's tantrum

Until
Worn out from it's thrashing
Tranquility is restored

Mist

Easing
Toward the sun

Mist
Dimming the far shore
Obscuring the trees and houses
Boats and docks

Mist
Reflecting the sun
With whitening particles

Mist
Dissolves as it
Slowly responds to
The soft breeze and
The warming sun

The Retreat

Five days
of
Humans B e i n g
silently together
Becoming
who they are

Five days of
Humans B e i n g
while sitting and walking
eating and working
sleeping and waking
Together

Five days of
Humans B e i n g
while laughing and crying
in awe and wonder
at the fluttering leaf
the mourning dove's whooo-whooo
the blue heron's wingspan
shadowing the sun
Watching at eventide
the white and red flashes of the storm

Five days of
Humans Being
Trying to be mindful of
Each breath

A breath in the ocean
of the air that
Caresses our skin
Gives life to our lungs
makes the planet green
and life exist
moment by moment

The Sandcastle

The sand waits

for the child with its shovel
digging into the water's edge
each shovel lifted into the bucket
then water added

Hand dipped into this magic mixture
watching each drip slowly
build upon another

Lost in time
the child
is embraced in the moment
of the castle's creation

The Breeze

Gently moving
Branches nodding
Leaves
     energetically swaying and trembling
moved by forces
Unseen

It Is Enough

The warming sun
The titmouse and the nuthatch
The scurrying squirrels
It is enough
To gladden my heart

Your hand in mine
Your smile when you see me
Your visible love
It is enough
To gladden my heart

The blooming crocus
The yellowing forsythia
The greening grass
It is enough
To gladden my heart

Your call "Can I visit?"
Your wonderful muffins
Our time spent together
It is enough
To gladden my heart

The spirit-calming music
The conversation about lessons
The deepness of your faith
The smiles on your faces
It is enough
To have me understand
The richness of our Morning Prayer

Grace before meals
The vibration of humming
Moments graced with silence
The rhythms of today
It is enough
To have me understand
The richness of our lives

The Mystery of Community

Community in Christ

Vulnerable
Open
Open to joy
Open to the wounds of
Friends and strangers
And Loved ones

Opening ourselves
Our unguarded selves
To share our ordinary lives
Touched by all the confusion and inconsistencies
Touched by grief and laughter
Touched by delight and wonder
Oft separated by only a breath

Is Peace Possible?

Can we
have the audacity to open
ourselves to peace?
Do we
have the courage
to understand it begins here in me
and in you?

Can we
have the boldness to believe
when we behold another with love
grace flows through us?

Can we
see the strength
in our brokenness?
It births compassion.

We are here together to hold one another,
to believe the impossible
is possible.
I reach out
and extend my hand to you
and say, "Yes".
This is the season of
light in the darkest days
when we celebrate love.

Born in a stable
at the Festival of Lights
a luminous star
lights up our world and shows us
that all impossibilities
are now imaginable.

Beholding the Countryside

I looked up from this paper
And saw
Trees
Standing perfectly still
The sky a muted blue
     Flowers in flower boxes
     Pink and yellow
       Flourishing and fading
      And
          Dead

In this moment
The trees
Are whispering to each other:
"We need rain!"
"Do you think the humans know
That in dry times
We need watering too?"

Picking up my pen
I write their words here
To share with you

Humanity

The understanding
That
Though we may look
Different from each other
Each human being
Is a blessing.
Each human being
Has gifts to offer humanity
Each human being
Is essential for the wholeness of humanity

In our journey to wholeness
Tears lead to our path's clarity
In our journey to wholeness
Hugs lift us over thresholds

We need
Someone
Anyone who believes
We are okay
Just as we are
Broken and flawed and weak
And in those attributes
We share our humanity

Holy, Holy, Holy

Lord of the universe
      and of me
Lord of stars and heavens
Lord of ants and elephants
      of hummingbirds and hawks
Lord of this planet earth
Show us the way

Teach us Christ's love
Christ's humanness
Christ's courage
Christ's vulnerability
Christ's tenderness

Teach us to listen
      then to understand
      then to act

Teach us to let go
      of hurt
      of narrow vision
      of needing to control

Teach us to hold on
      to each other
      to faith–knowing
      "I believe, help my unbelief"
      to friendship
      to our blessings
      to our pets

to our hopes
to our dreams
to our willingness to please you
to the magic of each day

Help us to be mindful of
squirrels flying
coyotes howling at night
bee and butterfly
the shy stranger

Help us to hear
music of frogs and birds
blending of human voices
melody of violin, guitar, piano, trumpet
flute and clarinet, bass drum
Cajun drum, cymbals and bells
harmonizing in perfect pitch
with your universe, Lord

Help us to see
what a rich tapestry of life
you designed for us, Lord
it is a spellbinding
world you have created,
for a trying and hopeful humanity

We thank you
for loving us
for forgiving us
for giving us countless opportunities
to return to your loving presence

Dragonfly

Flying   U
                        P

                 D
                 O
                 W
                 N

SIDEWAYS

                     Quick as a blink

……..Zip…….Zip…….Zip

                      Just like my mind

Beauty

Is your beauty
fragile
as a butterfly's wing
or bold
as the sleek leopard?

Are you drawn to
fragile or bold beauty?

Can something "ugly" be beautiful?
Can something beautiful
be ugly?

Can my eye behold beauty
in all nature
and in all of humankind?

How do you
how do I
decide
"Is this a thing of beauty?"

Do we even know
how we decide?

Candles

The gloom of today's rain
Crept into my spirit
                    Until
                        Molly called.
"I've lit candles all over my home!"
Her cheer glowed through the phone.
Now my home this day
                is warmed by candlelight,
The remembrance of Molly glowing through
        each flame.

Brown Leaves

Leaves,
Tall narrow oak and tri-edged maple
Blanket the deck.

I imagine their life reversing,
Floating back to their trees,
Turning yellow and red orange yellow,
And then green for most of their lives.

The reversion continues
Until they are
Barely perceptible nubs.

Those days are long past.
Now it is time
For their next evolution,
Giving themselves fully
To nourish the soil, plants and trees
For the succeeding spring's
Birds, butterflies and bees

Don't Tell Me

Don't tell me
how long healing will take

I cannot bear to hear
"weeks" or "months"

I cannot wait
and yet I do wait

to see the moments of
each day unfold and linger
awaiting
the gifts it will share
and at day's end
basking in gratitude for my many blessings

An Early Spring Morning

The taste of Irish oatmeal
        soft firm nubs
          mixed
with creamy yogurt and crunchy apple
        lingers in my mouth
    as I watch
    the titmouse and junco at the birdfeeder

    The trees in their soulful winter glory
      sway to the music of the wind

Dead leaves cling to the oak
        unwilling to let go
until spring comes and pushes them
    off the branch
        to make way for new life

And now
      a red bellied woodpecker
     enjoys the deserted feeder
    leaving it swinging as it takes flight

It is a gift to sit quietly and watch

Align

Again and again
let us align ourselves
with Love

With the sweetness
of Compassion, Kinship, and Community

Let us align ourselves with God's purpose
for each other and this earth

Fresh Eyes

When I wake
may my eyes
see
with a three year old's
excitement and wonder.

Sitting
back supported
by this Empire State oak,
feeling it's bark,
acorns soft and smooth
in my hand,
another and another envelop me
until my lap
is filled
with capped and capless acorns.

They embrace me
with faceless smiles
perceiving their surroundings.

I feel comforted.

A Peaceful Morning Moment

The deer
munching apples
the gift of the trees

A doe
        a fawn
                a young buck
chewing slowly
        jaws moving rhythmically
looking peaceful on our lawn
        yet ears alert to any sound

They bring such delight

filling me with a sense of serenity
as my eyes rest on them

I wonder
as they chew unhurriedly
if they feel the same calm

Grief

What do you say
when
there are no words
for the anguish
for the pain
for all the
"What ifs" that run
through your heart-brain?

What do you say?

You say nothing
Listen
in the silence
cry with her
cry for her
while she
needing strength
for her children
cannot cry – just yet

Cry for her and her children
and be
in this grief
sustaining your friend
in this intolerable, unfair
and incomprehensible time

Giving Thanks

This day as I
      put my warm feet on soft rug
I bow my head
I stand dressing warmly for this day
I put on my brace and
Grab my sturdy cane

I give thanks to the universe
For this new day
That I have never seen before

I give thanks for my frittata and coffee
The dishwasher
The running water
Both cold and hot

I give thanks for the sun streaming
Through the glass doors
Warming our home
And me

I give thanks
For the delightful view
Of the orange, red, yellow, and green leaves
On the trees and ground and
Swirling in the air

EMPTY

Of Self

I just looked at the word Empty and realized how close it is to the word Empathy – A and H added AH... AH... AH that is what it means to be Empty It means to have Empathy! It is at my core to understand others, to imagine myself in their shoes, to be them, to help know what makes them tick, what motivates and moves them in healthy and unhealthy ways.

From the age of 19 I remember having this passion to understand why a person would choose the path they did. Now I try to understand me; understanding me helps me have Empathy for others. In my poem "Happy Hoyden" it ends, "Because you are the last piece in the puzzle of me". Now I know that I am complete in myself.

What love does is make me realize my wholeness and see its vastness develop. It helps me to honor the challenges and welcome all who touch my life. It opens me to all the possibilities and opportunities of this life.

Happy Hoyden

With freckled dirt and bird nest crown
Streaking by a (hopefully blind) mother
Who won't see my
Rag bag jeans and (almost) polishing cloth jersey
But mother knew
And
Turning she saw
Only
My "I won" smile outshining the shiner
Bewildered teenager
Searching for answers and finding only more questions
Wanting
Needing to be part of something
Alone
Because
She was unwilling to compromise
What little she was sure of
Now a woman unaware of her metamorphosis
She fell in love with truth and spring
Knowledge and summer puddles
And still the rainbow had no pot of gold
Then
You loved me
Reality discarded fantasy's cloak
And I was whole
Because you are the last piece
Of the puzzle of me

Foster

Kindness

Compassion

Generosity

Foster Patience and Mindfulness

Foster Vision through eyes that cherish

Foster Friendship and Beauty

Foster Forgiveness of

Myself and others

Foster Love of

Others as well as myself

Foster a Willingness to say "I don't know"

Foster a Willingness to open the eyes my heart

Foster a Willingness to let go

Of the "need" to be right

Foster an Attitude that does not choke in my throat

When I say "I'm sorry"

Foster an Attitude of acceptance for unchangeable events and people

Foster an Attitude that opens our eyes to this day's awe

Foster the Wonder of curiosity

Foster the Wonder of the smell of the rain and texture of snow

The sight of the dawn breaking and the song of the birds waking

Foster the Wonder of the crescent moon and the morning star

Foster Gratitude for each loved one

Foster Gratitude for the flowers and

The birds & bees that pollinate them

Foster Gratitude for the sun and the rain and the air

In gratitude

"Every poem has poetry ancestors... No poem exists within a vacuum. There are always connections, probably ultimately to every poet in the world."
Joy Harjo, 23rd U.S.Poet Laureate

When I decided that I wanted to take some of the poems written over many years into a book, I thought of my friend Linda VanWagenen. She was an English teacher in her first years dedicated to education. She would be her teacher self and look at the poems with an analytical eye. And these poems reflect her input for which I'm most grateful. I am also thankful to have had Sandy Carlson's review of the poems her insight inspired another way to see.

Over the years here in Woodbury CT, I've gone to Molly Tate's journaling class at the library and Lin Northrup's writing class at the Senior Center. In Key West over the past 10 years I've had the opportunity to work with several authors at The Studios of Key West. They have each inspired me.

My husband Peter has always been supportive of my writing. In 2019 he built a small structure for me for my writing. It is green with red shutters and has 4 windows and of course a door. I've spent many happy hours there. It's called the Poet's Portal.

www.ingramcontent.com/pod-product-compliance
Lightning Source LLC
Chambersburg PA
CBHW022105020426

42335CB00012B/843